JEEZY

The Biography of Jeezy

University Press

CONTENTS

INTRODUCTION

I n 1998, rap was having a renaissance.

Nas, OutKast, Eminem, Missy Elliot, Jay-Z, Bone Thugs, Snoop Dog, Wu-Tang, Ice Cube, DMX, Tupac, Biggie. They had all debuted within the past few years, and their stars were rising.

Not a single one of them was sitting in the offices of the newest record label to open in Atlanta, Georgia.

It wasn't like they didn't know what they were doing, the man behind the desk mused. He and his partner, Demetrius Ellerbee – Kinky B, he went by professionally – knew what it took to make music that hit. He'd always had a feel for the beat, for the rhyme, for slinging out a lyric that snapped like a whip and cut to the bone. It was something that had to be felt, couldn't be taught, and he'd know it when he saw it.

If he ever saw it.

The label Corporate Thugz Entertainment – much later rebranded as CTE World – had signed on a few potentials. All locals are new to the game. He had hopes for them, but still. If he was going to make his mark on the world, he had to hustle. He had to focus.

It didn't help that the very first artist they'd signed had been recently arrested on a murder charge.

And there was no way he was going to miss out on making his mark on the world. He could see it now, a big dark signature right across the globe, telling everyone that Jay Wayne Jenkins was on the street, in the house, blowing it up.

But the artists he'd signed didn't seem to have the same vision, the same drive, that he had. They didn't share that pulsing in their head that moved him forward. Or they allowed themselves to get distracted by drink, drugs, and beef, which led to jail time. Street cred was everything in the world of rap and hip hop – street cred was king, street cred was meat and drink. Hard to convince a rapper that they ought to set aside their troubles with others and focus on their career. Apparently. With a wry shake of his head, he stared out the window at the streets of Atlanta passing him by.

"Ain't nobody gonna go as hard as you gonna go," he muttered to himself.

If the artists he'd signed didn't have the same hustle that he himself did, the obvious answer was staring him in the face. Forget being just the businessman behind the desk, trying to draw out talent where there was none. If he wanted the world, he had to go out and get it.

Up until then, surrounded by drink and drugs, with multiple run-ins with the law already under his belt at only twenty-one, he'd just been trying to survive.

But by the time he was done, he swore to himself everyone would know his name.

CHAPTER 1

The autumn of 1977 in Columbia, South Carolina, was as stiflingly hot as usual. The city was bustling, the second largest in the state, with a population of well over 100,000. Being pregnant and then in labor in the sweltering, highly humid heat wasn't for the faint of heart, but there wasn't a thing that Sandra Jenkins could do about it.

Besides, this wasn't her first rodeo. She already had a small son, Michael. As tumultuous as her relationship with her children's father was, she thanked God for the privilege of bringing another precious life into the world.

It wasn't going to be easy for either one of them, but it would be worth it.

The baby was born on September 28th. High noon and hot. Healthy, crying, already the image of his mother from the moment he took his first breath. She named him Jay – Jay Wayne Jenkins.

Jay's start in life was just about as difficult as his mother had feared. His parent's marriage was troubled, had been from the get-go; things were rendered even worse when his older brother Michael, still little more than an infant himself, died unexpectedly. The tragedy only deepened the rift between Jay's parents, though Jay himself was too young to remember much about his older sibling.

Though their life together in Columbia was neither simple nor easy, it was still hard to leave it behind when the time came. Their cheap little apartment was further filled when Jay's younger sister, Katrina. Money was hard to come by, a problem exacerbated by the fact that both halves of the young couple had picked up the same habits that so many around them had – drugs and alcohol, quickly leading to dependency. It made work hard to find and even harder to keep. At the end of his rope, Jay's father turned to the only sure source of income he could find and joined the army.

The little Jenkins family was cut loose from Columbia, from South Carolina entirely. They moved around, hopping from base to base with Jay's father at times, spending other times back in Georgia with Sandra's extensive family. Before he was ten years old, Jay had lived in Atlanta, Macon, and Hawkinsville, as well as stints in Japan when he was small and then in Hawaii. Wherever he went, he figured out a hustle. He had nothing; nobody was going to do him any favors or give him anything for free. Jay was a smart kid with a wide, warm smile and a quick way with words. He could talk his way into anything – but talking his way out of it could be more tricky.

Life at home wasn't a cakewalk, either. His parents were always fighting; he was very close with his mother and younger sister, but his father's habits and method of raising children were the source of endless clashes between all family members. Sandra Jenkins worked hard to raise her children as best as she could in an unstable environment. She took on housecleaning jobs, anything to supplement the income from the army. She believed in tough love and always encouraged her kids to get more from life than they had been given – a lesson Jay took to heart.

As he grew up on the base, he saw his main problem as a lack of finances. His parents still had nothing apart from his father's income, and that was used up as soon as the check showed. Jay applied his mind to the problem and soon found that he could steal and smuggle items off the base to send back to the contiguous States to sell. It all worked smoothly for a while, and he used the money to fund his burgeoning habits, much like his parents. There wasn't a lot else to do. The school was a matter of choice, not necessity, and attendance was hit-and-miss. He played some with his younger sister Trina, but most of his time was spent on the streets of whatever town, state, or country he lived in at the time.

But a thieving kid can only get away with things for so long before the adults catch on. When the officers at the base realized what the Jenkins boy was up to, he was unceremoniously jettisoned from life on the base and sent back to live with his grandmother in Georgia.

On the streets of Atlanta, back in the hood, Jay joined his cousins in investigating the new possibilities and opportunities that had opened up here: not just getting his own fix, but dealing. Dealing was a surefire way of making money, far better than stealing, smuggling, and selling stuff from the base. He was only eleven years old, not old or big enough for the older sellers or users to take him seriously. He quickly found that the fastest way to make his mark was to act like a middleman, even though he was the seller himself.

He made friends and connections quickly, greeting every new acquaintance as though they'd known each other forever. When they asked about getting some product, he would offer to go and collect it for them if they gave him the money upfront.

"Then I'd just go back to my grandma's house, eat some cereal," he recalled much later on. "Then bring them back the bag like I'd gone to get it, but I had it myself all the time."

It was tricky, but it worked, and at eleven years old, Jay had a steady flow of income from dealing. He would deal in the early morning, then go home for breakfast before going to middle school. He provided for his uncles, cousins, and other family members. He picked up on the signs that a drug bust was in the works; he learned to avoid scenes with ice cream trucks, as cops would hide in them to avoid detection until they could leap out and nab the culprits. His grandmother seemed unaware of her young grandson's burgeoning career. Jay loved his grandmother, despite – or perhaps because of – her seeming innocence. More than anyone he had ever met, she was a firm believer in the importance of rose-colored glasses, of looking for the good in everyone and seeing value everywhere. She treated him well; though her daughter's belief in tough love had been handed down in the family, Jay's grandmother never let him forget that she loved him and that he had value. It was a lesson that stayed with him, though he would not find a way to articulate it until decades later.

For a while, everything seemed copacetic.

Then came the news from the base. The strained, troubled relationship between his parents was finally coming to an end. His mother was coming home.

CHAPTER 2

Of all the terms that Jay Jenkins could use to describe his childhood, the one he settled on is "empty."

He filled his days. Dealing was fast, but it wasn't easy. When his mother moved back to Georgia, she found them a single-wide trailer to live in herself, Jay, and Katrina. The trailer cost $3500, and Sandra didn't have the money since her main income had been through Jay's father. Jay went to work and quickly hustled the amount, ready to hand over to buy the trailer. His mother, who had her own history with drugs – a history which was continuing at the time, though Jay didn't know it – was suspicious of where he got the money.

Jay was also helping his uncle with his roofing business now and then and passed it off as though he had simply saved up the funds from that side business. Unlike Jay's grandmother, though, his mother caught on almost immediately to the fact that her son was mixed up with drugs and made it clear that this was unacceptable.

"At the time, we bumped heads a lot," Jay recalled later. "I was learning who I was, and I was in the streets at a young age, so – she wasn't cool with that."

The closest relationships can cause the deepest pain, and it was both heartbreaking and infuriating to Jay that he couldn't seem to get on an even keel with his mother, who had been the center of his life for so long. But his natural stubbornness evidently came from her side, and neither of them was about to back down.

Eventually, Jay's mother gave him an ultimatum: either abide by her rules while he lived under her roof or go back to live with his grandmother. Unwilling to give up the hustle that had proven to be lucrative for him, which had paid for the trailer his mother was living in, he returned to his grandmother's house.

It was then, with his father out of the picture and his relationship with his mother strained to the limit, that reality hit him. Jay Jenkins realized that he had to fend for himself.

Dealing still seemed to be the best way. He'd practically fallen into it, and as he reached his mid-teens, he knew he was good at it. Tough enough, ballsy enough. He'd had a few run-ins with the cops, but nothing he couldn't handle. At fifteen, still in school, the world was his on a platter.

That view changed in a second – a razor-sharp reality check second – when he found his mother passed out in a crack den.

It was a shock that made him get the shakes like ice-cold water had been dumped all over him. He knew that his mother had done drugs in the past; he had vague memories of it as a child, even, and had wondered whether the presence of drugs in the house had led to how easily he'd gotten into dealing. But he had never seen her like this, like a sick shell of herself. The shock quickly gave way to fury; he couldn't decide whom he hated more, his mother for allowing this to be done to her or the dealers who had given her the means. With another cold wash of shock and shame, he realized he was one of them.

Dealing had seemed his way out of the trap he'd been born into, but it was taking his mother out at the same time.

The realization hit home. But thinking of getting out of dealing was much easier said than done; in the end, he made the painful decision to cut ties with his mother for a time. Every time he looked at her, all he could see was the slack, empty, vacant expression that she'd had in the crack house. Their relationship had been strained; now, they were estranged. Trying to forget the shock of what he'd seen, Jay threw himself into business. But just as he had found when he was kicked off the base in Hawaii, he couldn't outrun the consequences of what he was doing forever. In 1994, at seventeen years old, it was more than just dodging the cops and getting a slap on the wrist. Caught with narcotics in his possession, he was sent to the Youth Challenge Academy in Fort Stewart, Georgia. Affiliated with the base at Fort Stewart, the YCA was a boot camp for troubled kids or, more specifically, kids who caused trouble. Jay Jenkins spent nine months there, the last little bit of his "childhood," turning eighteen as he launched himself back on the streets. His father had been in the military. He didn't want any part of it.

The one thing that he kept from his time at the YCA was a friend he made. Demetrius Ellerbee was also doing time at the boot camp, and the two fell in together, drawn by a mutual drive to take the world by storm, to pursue the high-living lifestyle they'd always dreamed of by any means necessary.

Around that time, Jay moved back to live in Macon, Georgia. Resettling into his hustle, he found it was just as easy as ever to make friends out on the streets. He befriended many local members of the Crips, later even affiliating himself with the gang for a time; it helped his street cred, and street cred was everything. Everybody knew that. Anyone who said any different just didn't have any.

His friendship with Ellerbee continued, and the two began to talk about going into business together.

They each had their own hustle, but combining their resources was a lucrative proposition. At eighteen, Jay suddenly had a partner.

The hustle continued, but Ellerbee had his eye on other things. Music was important to both young men, rap, and hip-hop, the steady beat and the rapid-fire lyrics fueled them to get up, and the day pounded through their nights. It was the sound of their generation, the sound of the hood, the sound of their identity. It was the only kind of music telling the stories of people like them. There was an authenticity to it, creating a culture where living the lyrics was the only way to earn respect. But it wasn't enough; Ellerbee, in particular, was dissatisfied with what he was hearing on the radio. It was too safe, too mainstream. It had so much further to go if the artists would just push it past its limits.

It was his idea, initially, to form a record label.

"If they can do it," he told Jay, jerking his head at the thumping radio, "we can do it."

Between the two of them, they had the stakes to get started. Jay had never considered a music career, but the idea was immediately appealing. It wasn't a way out of dealing; it was just a supplement, a hobby. But music fit in well with the lifestyle he'd been seeking. Running a record label was a new way to hold the world in his hands. He was on board.

In the ever-changing realm of hip-hop and rap,

with new subgenres appearing just about every month, the producers behind the sounds were just as important, most of the time, as the artists who were making the sounds themselves. Producing was a comfortable niche for Jay. He didn't mind sitting in the recording studio or sitting behind a desk.

At least, not at first.

As the first few months swept by, the very newness of the venture was enough to keep him hooked. He and Ellerbee went out on the streets, going to local venues to shop the talent that was available in Atlanta. But just like Ellerbee had been disappointed with what he heard on the radio, Jay was disappointed with what he heard on the stages at the local dives. He, too, could sense the scope for change that was facing rap and hip-hop, and he wanted to do something more than what was already being done.

But a record label wasn't a record label unless it was doing some recording, so they signed their first hopeful – who was almost immediately arrested and moved out of Atlanta to face a murder charge.

Back to the beginning, CTE was left without an artist to record and promote. Jay and Ellerbee had already rented a studio – a studio that was just an empty space, as it turned out, so they had to furnish all the equipment for themselves, too. Money had been invested. They couldn't turn back now.

The answer was clear to Ellerbee.

"Why don't you do it?" he asked Jay.

Jay's quickness with words, his understanding of telling a narrative within a song, and his charisma and the street cred he'd already racked up made him a natural choice for the first artist to be released by CTE. But at first, he demurred.

"I'm not a rapper."

And he wasn't – until suddenly he was.

The combination of a lack of signable talent willing to hustle and his own boredom with sitting behind the desk like a respectable businessman led Jay to play around in the recording booth. With his undeniable talent for putting words together on the spot, he improvised a few lyrics, throwing in off-the-cuff asides that would become a signature performing method.

Between Ellerbee's encouragement and his own realistic assessment of the facts – coupled with his never-ending drive – Jay quickly decided to set the business aspect of the record label aside for the moment and focus on actually producing a product.

He wasn't about to release his first album as Jay Wayne Jenkins, though. In 2001, Jay's debut independent album, *Thuggin' Under the Influence (TUI)*, was released under his first nom de rap, Lil J. drawing on his ability to make friends in the business – any business he set his mind to – the album featured contributions from Ellerbee and rappers Freddy J., and Lil Jon, among others; Lil Jon also served as a producer on the project.

Whether he saw himself as a rapper or not, Jay Jenkins was off and running.

CHAPTER 3

In the early 2000s, the only thing that matched the speed with which Jay's popularity grew was the speed of his ambition. Ambition for his company, ambition for his friends, ambition for himself.

Two years after the release of his first album, in 2003, Jay released his second independent album, a two-CD set called Come Shop with Me. Drawing on the underground hit he'd already made, the album was more of the style that was quickly becoming his signature, featuring several new tracks as well as some remixes of songs that had already been hit on TUI.

Still not seeing himself primarily as a rapper, Jay still found that writing the lyrics for his songs was a way to not only express himself but to explore himself. Street cred was everything; he'd lived what a lot of rappers only rapped about. He had more street cred in his little finger than half the big-name artists out there. He had more of a story to tell, and every word of it came from someone who knew. From the beginning, his lyrics centered on the lifestyle he had come from, compared to the lifestyle he was reaching for with every successful sale and deal.

Later, the subgenre he helped to popularize and codify became called trap. A trap was an abandoned house used to deal, peddling drugs to the users who crawled out of their own dens to find their next fix. A trap was the sort of place he'd found his mother in years before, but he always pushed the thought away as soon as it came. Traps were the source of his income from childhood, the last-gasp attempt to make a living and take care of himself and the ones he loved. It was easy to hate them; the trouble was he had to respect them, too, for giving him and so many others a start. For giving him and many like him a chance to stave off starvation for another day.

Trap as a subgenre, understandably, came from a complex and difficult-to-define place. If you hadn't lived it, you couldn't talk about it.

Last resort and first port of call for everyone on the way down, whether dealer or user. In 1998, the same year Jay started CTE, OutKast wrote lyrics about trap houses.

"So now you are back at the trap, just that, trapped.

Go on and marinate on that for a minute."

The trap was markedly different from the genre

of rap. Where the tracks that Jay had grown up with focused on a lifestyle of excess, of diamonds and gold and bling and glitter, the trap was about the down and out, the struggle to survive – and the triumph that was all the greater when you succeeded. But in the early days of Jay's career as an artist, he was still juggling the aftermath of his career as a dealer, unwilling to let the lucrative door close completely.

It was a new friend, rapper T.I., who convinced him otherwise.

As he was working on an upcoming album in the studio, the rapper stopped by to see how the project was coming. Jay was in the booth, but he had a stash there with him. TI beckoned to him.

"Come here. I wanna talk to you in private."

In the men's bathroom at the studio, TI gave him some of the most simple and yet the most life-changing advice from someone who had been in his shoes.

"Look, you can try to do music and drugs, but that only lasts so long. You gotta choose one or the other."

Jay laughed at him.

"Look who's talking. Don't you do both?"

"Hell, no! I left that alone a long time ago."

Later, Jay recounted, "For me, it was a real wake-up call." The fact that TI knew what he was talking about, that he'd stood in Jay's shoes not that long before and come through, gave his words more weight than they would have had otherwise. He wasn't the only one who had asked Jay to give up the lifestyle of a dealer; his grandmother, his mother, his sister, and his exes all had done the same at one point or another. But the way TI put it gave him another perspective: it wasn't all or nothing with dealing. It was a choice of one thing or another. One way of surviving – drugs – or another – music.

He didn't have to give up on everything all at once, anyhow, he figured. TI's words stuck with him, but change is a process, not a light switch.

In 2004, Jay's career took a huge leap forward. On the back of the success of his first two independent albums, he began to be courted by other labels; notably, the first was Bad Boy Records, founded eleven years earlier by Sean Combs, Puff Daddy himself. Bad Boy Records was an imprint of Epic Records, a division of Sony Music Entertainment. Bad Boy and Combs had released albums from artists such as the Notorious BIG; Combs had also produced and developed projects for artists like Mary J. Blige and Usher. By signing with Bad Boy Records, Jay was stepping into a whole new level of fame and opportunity.

That same year, Jay joined a group of other Atlanta locals and became a member of the *Boyz n da Hood* roster along with fellow artists Jody Breeze, Gorilla Zoe, Big Gee, and Big Duke. The Southern gangsta rap group released their self-titled debut under Bad Boy Records label in 2005; the debut hit number five on the Billboard 200 album chart.

At the same time as he was stretching his wings and gaining street cred with the Boyz, Jay's demo was being shopped around on his behalf by Henry Lee, who managed Jazze Pha. Lee brought it to Shakir Stewart, then the Vice President of Artist and Repertoire at Def Jam Recordings. Def Jam had a decades-long history of signing hit artists and producing hit albums, from LL Cool Jay and the Beastie Boys to Public Enemy and Slayer and DMX. Stewart "fell in love" with the demo and took it to L.A. Reid, the CEO of Def Jam, who agreed that Jay had talent and should be brought into the Def Jam fold. By that point, Jay's independent albums combined with his stint with the *Boyz n da Hood* had garnered him enough attention and respect that other record labels came hunting – Interscope Records and Warner Records among them. Jay had his pick of where he wanted to take his career next.

In the end, he shook hands with Reid and Steward and signed on with Def Jam.

CHAPTER 4

2005 was a good year for Jay Jenkins' career – a big year.

In July of that year, his first major label album was released. *Let's Get It: Thug Motivation 101*. The album was produced through Jay's own CTE, which now worked under the distribution of Def Jam Recordings. The popularity of the album meant popularity – and continued solvency – for CTE, too. Jay was making waves not only as an artist but as the businessman and record producer he'd started out to be.

Thug Motivation 101 debuted at number two on the Billboard charts, selling almost 200,000 copies in the very first week, Jay's first top ten debut. The numbers followed through, and it went platinum in its first month; in 2020, the album was certified as double platinum. Suddenly, Jay Jenkins – Young Jeezy, as an artist – was hot stuff. A decade later, hip-hop writer Brooklyn Russell said that, with his first album, Jay laid down "the blueprint for an entire region of rappers."

Somewhere between signing on with Bad Boy Records and the release of *Thug Motivation 101*, his life as a dealer had given way to life as a talented artist. TI's advice had stuck with him, and he'd made the choice to walk away from the street life he'd led and embrace his new career.

It was not a choice that could be made lightly. Street cred was still king, and some of his friends who had grown up in the same streets as he did made fun of him for what they saw as turning his back on his childhood, his heritage, his foundation in life. The trap had been an opportunity for him; what kind of fake persona was he putting on by denying it?

But he wasn't denying it; he was just trying to let it be a part of his past rather than his present.

All the same, he got used to being laughed at.

It became a little less funny when many of his inner circle began to see their past catch up with them at last. Some of them had been through similar experiences as Jay – boot camps, juvenile hall, slaps on the wrist. But they weren't kids anymore. One by one, many of his oldest friends started to go down— possession, dealing, gunfights, robbery, murder.

"The minute everyone started getting indicted is when I started blowing up," he would later recall. "I was like, 'Damn, I'm supposed to be here.'"

Another factor that played into his decision to focus on life in the recording studio rather than the streets was his family. As difficult as it had been growing up, he still had close relationships with his grandmother, his sister, and even the cousins that had introduced him to dealing way back when. Their seemingly unconditional love was almost shaming.

"It's hard going through your day knowing how your family feels about you. You're in gunfights and all kinds of dumb shit, and they're still calling you, like, 'Are you okay?' And thinking of getting caught and doing real-time – you don't want that on your conscience when you know you had a chance."

With the drive and hustle that had characterized him since he was a kid, Jay Jenkins seemed to have more of a chance than others who had grown up the same way.

All the same, watching his old friends get arrested and put away behind bars hit him hard. He had always made friends easily and treasured the people in his life, even when they disagreed. Though his career was taking off, he remembers that time as being a very dark period in his life, one where he turned to smoking and drinking to dull the pain of realization – the realization of how close he had come to being in prison himself. The realization of how close he had come to throwing all his potential away.

Jay walked a fine line between the tug and pull of his past life and the glitter of the new one. His history was given a sheen by his popularity and success as a rapper; it would have been easy to fall into the same rut that so many other rappers had become prey to, releasing unauthentic music that focused on the highs and excesses of their lifestyle rather than what life was really about. He wasn't interested in that. The trap was starting to cross over into other genres, getting heard, getting played. It was reality rap.

At the same time, Jay had bigger things in mind for his career – bigger aims, even then. He told an interviewer, "I don't just do music for the clubs; I do music for the struggle. I do music for the kids who ain't got no sense of direction."

Real and gritty, drastic and gripping, he wanted his music to guide the kids raised on the streets and tell them that there was something better out there. They just had to find it – just like he had – and it was going to take a hustle.

CHAPTER 5

J ay's popularity was such that he was now called on to be featured on tracks by other artists. Chief among them, Boyz n da Hood's Dem Boyz, though he had left the group behind when he signed with Def Jam as a solo artist. Another heavy-hitter feature was on Gucci Mane's So Icy.

Gucci Mane – or Radric Delantic Davis, as he had been born – was a few years younger than Jay and came from the same type of background as Jay himself. His debut album was *Trap House*, and together with Jay and a handful of others, he was turning trap music into a popular subgenre. *So Icy* was his breakout hit; at the time, it was also seen as a breakout hit for Jay, as well, and ended up leading to a long-standing beef between the two. *So Icy* was produced for Gucci Mane's album *Trap House*, but Jay had a partial writing credit and felt that he had a stake in the song as well. On top of that, he felt that he was underpaid and under-credited for his part in the recording and production of the song. Taking advantage of the opportunity to attach his name to it more directly, he offered to buy the rights to the song outright for inclusion on his own album, Thug Motivation 101. He took this offer to the producer, Zaytoven, who turned him down. Gucci Mane resented the fact that Jay made the offer at all. Later, he and his camp appeared to suggest that gang members from Macon – the Crips that Jay had made friends with years before – attacked Gucci Mane and his entourage on Jay's behalf. The truth of the matter remained up for debate, though, with Gucci Mane's own history – his debut album was released on the same day he was bonded out on murder charges, for example – most figured he could handle himself either way. When Jay wrote a lyric later that year putting a $10,000 bounty on the chain that Gucci Mane wore, it only added to the fire.

Jay wasn't exactly squeaky clean, himself. Though he had turned his back on dealing and tried to make his life over again, the associates he kept and the situations he got involved with drew the attention of the police. In early 2006, he and some of his friends were arrested following an alleged shootout in Miami Beach, Florida. He was charged with two counts of carrying a concealed weapon. However, two months later, shortly before *Thug Motivation 101* debuted, the charges were dropped due to a lack of evidence. Though the word had gotten out that he'd walked away from the drug scene, such was the power of street cred that the occasional dust-up with law enforcement only added to his authenticity.

But that wasn't what Jay was about – at least, not entirely. As he grew older and began to realize the impact that fame could have on a man, the lessons he'd learned from his grandmother earlier in his life came back to him. She had always taught him that everyone had value, that he should treat others as he wanted to be treated, and that when you treated someone with love, they were sent out into the world as better people. As someone who'd had a rough upbringing on the brink of poverty, with a childhood darkened by violence and drugs, he was far from the minority – and he felt a strong sense of solidarity with others who had suffered in similar ways.

Not just those who had similar upbringings but those who had what little they possessed taken from them through no fault of their own.

In 2001, Jay founded the Street Dreamz Foundation, a non-profit organization designed to provide aid and support to underserved and underprivileged children, encouraging "a generation of at-risk youth to become effective leaders through programs that foster independence and respect for others while educating and motivating each child to reach their ultimate potential in their area of interest," as the mission statement laid out. As his life changed for the better, Jay wanted to not only reach forward but to reach back, helping the communities that had raised him to be the man he became. Working with the foundation to make a difference for others became a major goal in his life, one which continues to be a priority even now.

Jay found himself even more stirred to action when witnessing the suffering of others. In late August 2005, Hurricane Katrina made landfall in Florida, devastating the Gulf Coast. Watching the aftermath, the loss of life and property, Jay was horrified and depressed to see what had happened to thousands of people. As a native of the South, it hit home – and it hit hard.

"At the end of the day," he said in an interview later that year, "it's our people in need of help. This is the same place I did a gang of shows, the same people who supported me over the years. You're talking about a place we used to go to support the Super Bowl, and it's like a Third World country now. There's a bond. I'm an Atlanta dude; I look at it like it could've been us. It could have been my people living in the Georgia Dome trying to survive."

It was when talking with rapper Lil Wayne, a native of New Orleans, that Jay was moved to take action. When told that the rapper hadn't had a chance to connect with his mother or his son, it hurt Jay's heart. By this point, he had a son of his own, Jadarius Jenkins, with Tadisha Dykes; he couldn't imagine what it must be like not to be able to reach out to his boy and make sure he was okay. He had a large house in Atlanta, big enough to fit twelve or fourteen people, and offered it as a place for Lil Wayne to stay if he needed it.

Wayne turned him down, but Jay took the idea and ran with it instead of leaving it to lie there. He opened up his home to others – complete strangers, those in need. It was a serious responsibility, a duty.

"How we handle this is going to set the tone for the future," he said later on. "This is one of the times we've got to come together. There are like 14 people in my crib I've never seen a day before in my life, but I ain't tripping. They can stay as long as they need. This could be the end of some people's roads. We've got to help people start to rebuild their lives."

Opening his home wasn't enough, either. He started to spread the word around Atlanta, calling on his fellow Georgians to contribute food and clothing, water, baby formula, and diapers to send to the Gulf Coast. In the end, his efforts resulted in a round dozen eighteen-wheeler trucks carting tons of supplies down to those in need. Later, he joined an all-star roster in a charity concert for the Heal the Hood Foundation.

Near the end of 2007, along with CTE, Jay started a week-long toy drive for underprivileged kids, hoping to provide some joy in the Christmas season. The drive ended in providing a thousand toys to a thousand children. As he worked along with his friends and other celebrities – and along with normal, everyday working-class folks who had the same goal that he did – Jay couldn't help but think of his own childhood, of stealing cell phones and other electronics from the base to sell for money to get what he wanted. No one had ever been able to give him his desires as a gift. He'd worked hard for them all.

If he could do anything, he promised himself he'd make sure that none of the kids he could help would ever have an empty childhood.

CHAPTER 6

J ay's next few albums stayed in line with the preceding releases, providing him with an unbroken series of successes – and consecutive number-one albums. His third studio album, The Recession, saw him working with Kanye West, earning Jay his first Grammy Award nomination for Best Rap Performance by a Duo.

Around the same time, in 2007, Jay founded a new group with two other rappers, USDA. Their first album, Cold Summer, peaked at number four on the US charts, number one on the US rap list. The next year, 2008, Jay was honored with the BET Hip Hop Award, as well as garnering two Ozone awards for two consecutive years.

Jay continued appearing elsewhere and featuring on tracks for other artists: Akon's *I'm So Paid*, Usher's *Love in this Club*, and Ciara's *Never Ever*, among them. His gruff, rather growling tone was instantly recognizable, and his sharp wit and playfully blunt energy were in high demand among his peers.

His sharp wit and blunt energy made him a fascinating person to watch in other arenas, including politics. Jay heavily identified with and championed Barack Obama, who announced his bid for President of the United States in February 2007. The undeniable effects of systemic racism had impacted Jay throughout his life; Black artists dominated his chosen field, but he was all too keenly aware that this was not in itself an evident proof of equality or fairness. By his own telling, he never paid much attention to politics; in the centuries that the United States had existed, nobody could deny that Blacks had been shunted to the side. He saw the political arena as something that didn't matter much to him, one way or another, as a Black man.

However, with President Obama setting a new standard, politics got his attention. In 2009, Jay and Jay-Z performed together in a concert to celebrate Obama's inauguration. Jay had written a piece called *My President is Black*; it was hardly a surprise when this drew the ire of – predominantly white – critics.

"This time around, it's not a black-or-white thing. You got somebody in there for us that's well-spoken and going to handle their business," Jay said in response. "I just wanted to do my part and let them know we need change; we need help; it's rough out there." Directly addressing one particular critic of the performance, Bill O'Reilly, Jay said thoughtfully,

"I don't think he really understands my struggle."

From someone who kept his political opinions to himself to someone who spoke out in favor of change, Jay continued to evolve his persona to fit the changing times – all while doing his best to stay true to his roots and keep what street cred he'd racked up over the years. Part of the metamorphosis that he underwent – a metamorphosis that was almost expected in the hip-hop world – was the alteration of his name.

He'd already done it once, changing the name he initially was credited by – Lil J – to Young Jeezy. But in 2010, the rumor started to spread that he was, in turn, dropping the "young" from Young Jeezy. Jay quickly contradicted the rumor, but the cover for his single *Lose My Mind* listed him as Jeezy anyway. Whether Jay started the rumor himself or the rumor made him start thinking about a change, it was later, in 2013, that it finally came true.

"It sounds good because when I came in the game, that's who I was, and that was my state of mind," he said ruefully in an interview on RapFix Live. "But I'm a grown man. Those zeros get to adding up, you gotta drop the 'young.'"

Around the time that he evidently had started thinking about becoming just Jeezy, Jay also struggled with an ailment that almost certainly made him feel older than his years. In 2010, at the age of thirty-three, in the middle of a video shoot, he was struck with Bell's Palsy. Shortly before that, the single *Lose My Mind* had already been released to whet people's appetites for Jay's upcoming album, *Thug Motivation 103*. *Lose My Mind* hit hard, becoming Jay's fifth single to reach the Top 40 and earning him his third Grammy nomination. But the album release had to be pushed back while Jay recovered from his bout with Bell's and was not released until 2011.

Jay knew that he was not the young man who had started out his career with a carefree, impromptu attempt at rap lyrics. Life as a hardcore rapper, especially one with real street cred, was not geared toward longevity. He was in his mid-30s. By this point, he had two children. He'd already walked away from the life he had assumed would kill him in the end. But as he grew older, he found that he was finally beginning to understand how much there was left to live for.

In order to achieve it, he would have to continue to adapt. To be a survivor.

To not let anything – not even himself – stand in his way.

CHAPTER 7

P art of adapting to his new priorities meant accepting his role as a father.

Another part of it meant accepting his role as a son.

In 2014, Jay had a daughter with his then-girlfriend, musician Mahlet Gebregiorgis. They named the little girl Amra Nor Jenkins, and Jay found himself once again falling hard. Later, he would post a tribute to his toddler daughter: "Since the 1st day you were born, I've been a better man, individual, and father."

Being a father didn't necessarily soften Jay, but there was no denying that it did something. With a lifetime of focus on himself and the hustle, it gave him a new dimension as a man. As radio personality Incognito would say later, "We've all witnessed the growth in Jeezy. In life, that's what it's all about, is evolving and going to the next level. This is the guy that came in telling us to trap or die, and now we're watching him as a father. We're watching him expand."

Jay would later express how much he treasured the fact that his mother had always encouraged him to follow his dreams and had never looked down on them. Still, he was definite about what he did not want for his children: a career in rap and hip-hop. In 2015, he outright stated that he didn't want his kids to follow in his footsteps. The oldest of his children, Jadarius Jenkins, instead chose an alternate path, attending college to gain an education in fashion and design in order to launch a clothing line. Jay's younger son, Shyheim, and daughter, Amra, have so far chosen to stay out of the spotlight as much as possible, which Jay has done his best to make easy for them to achieve.

As Jay grew older – as he grew up – he was glad to welcome his mother back into his life.

Sandra's life had hit rock bottom some years before, around the time that Jay split paths with her after finding her in the trap house. After years of hard work, sweat, tears, relapses, and pain, she had finally gotten clean. Their reunion was emotional; Jay couldn't help but vividly remember how much he had loved and idolized his mother as a young boy.

It saddened him to realize just how much both of them had missed out on, all because of the choices they had both made and the circumstances that they were thrown into.

When he left home, he said, "I took a lot of my time trying to come up, trying to take care of everybody. I didn't really take the time to be a son. Now, when I see people moving around taking their mothers on tour or on vacation, doing things, it's like, damn, I gotta go see my mother in this place. It hurt because I missed all that time. I can't get any of it back. I didn't get anything but some money, so I didn't really gain much. I lost my mom, but I thank her every day for giving me morals."

Ultimately, despite the lost time, he was proud of his mother for fighting through the black hole of her addiction and working with him to rebuild their relationship. "It was painful, but at the same time, it taught me a valuable lesson in life. People can be the way they are, but as long as they're willing to change — that's what you've got to look at."

Jay not only recognized the importance of adapting within himself but in others. His grandmother had taught him that everyone had value, even when they disappointed him. With his mother back in his life and close relationships with his sister and cousins, he could look back at their shared past and be grateful for what he had.

"Everything I've ever done has been about evolution," he said, years later, looking back. And every moment of evolution had led him toward something better.

CHAPTER 8

J ay's ninth album was planned to be his last. He announced it that way, to the consternation of his fans. He had a new goal in mind: acting.

He was far from the first rapper to want to add acting to his repertoire. Will Smith, Ice Cube, LL Cool J, Queen Latifah – there was something about the stage and drama of rap and hip hop that seemed to mesh well with the theatrics of Hollywood, whether on the big screen or on television. Later that year, Jay racked up his first film credit with *I Got the Hook Up 2*. The experience quickly settled his need to launch into the film industry – at least for the time being – and he returned his sights to music the next year, coming out of his brief retirement without missing a beat.

He was continuing to evolve, but sometimes the way forward was also the way back.

Throughout his career, he had crafted lyrics that

were reflective of the times the world was going through. In 2008, his album The Recession had been almost celebratory, despite hard economic times; Barack Obama was the first Black president, and things were looking up. Twelve years later, amid a worldwide pandemic in 2020, with Trump in office and the United States more divided than ever, his comeback album was deeply connected to that time in a way that almost mirrored it. He titled it *The Recession 2*.

"When I wrote the last Recession," Jay commented, "we were celebrating. Barack Obama was coming into office. Things were different. It wasn't this bad. So this is a different feel." He found himself inspired to touch on the difficult times they were going through as a nation, as a world, "but at the same time, motivate my people and give them something to help them through these times and to celebrate because the shift is happening. You're either going to come out of this better or worse, better or bitter. For me, I wanted to come out of it better."

But the theme of *The Recession 2* was not the only throwback that Jay had in store around the release of the album. On the night before it was launched to the public, mere hours before critics began to comb through the lyrics, the themes, the beats, years' worth of butting heads publicly came to a very public finish when Jay and Gucci Mane, his one-time collaborator – and nemesis ever since – met for an installment of Verzuz.

Verzuz was the brainchild of producers Timbaland and Swizz Beatz. Born of the pandemic and illustrative of how deeply creative creators could get when they were stuck inside, the webcast was a series of battles between artists. Centered on the concept of competitive streaming, each battle would consist of up to twenty rounds, taking hours at a time, with each artist playing their greatest hits – back to back. For some, it was used as a springboard for publicity, a way to tease and joke with their fellow artists and friends.

For Jay and Gucci Mane, it was the culmination of years of animosity.

Though they had met way back in 2005, their brief collaboration on the single *So Icy* had been the highlight of their acquaintance. From there, Gucci Mane's anger with Jay's attempt to buy the single had only expanded. The tension was not helped when Jay turned down the request to perform *So Icy* in concert with Gucci Mane – a detail from the past that was not revealed until a documentary about Jay's career was released years later. At the time, Jay was on bed rest after surgery for throat polyps; whether Mane didn't believe him or simply didn't accept this as a good enough reason, their enmity only grew from there.

Not long after, Gucci Mane was at the home of a friend when a group of strangers burst in unexpectedly. Mane shot and killed one of the group in what he claimed later was self-defense – a claim that was upheld in court. The man he'd shot was Henry Lee Clark, known as Pookie Loc, a close associate and friend of Jay Jenkins.

For years afterward, rumors circulated that Jay was the one who had set up the home invasion just to get back at Gucci Mane, accidentally sending his friend to his death in the process. Jay had always denied it, and the idea that so many believed he would willingly do such a thing – and be the cause of Pookie's death – horrified him. Gucci Mane was one of the main instigators behind the rumor, further adding to the animosity between the two men.

With more than ten years of distrust and outright enmity between the two, it was no surprise that a sizable crowd tuned in to watch their Verzuz session – more than five million, all told.

And none of them were disappointed. The rap battle was, as one outlet put it, "actually a battle." Between the hits, which flew fast and furious, the two traded barbed quips and sharp commentary, their entire history laid out for the world to see.

"My outfit cost 10 bands," Mane said, jeering at Jay's clothing. "Look at my opponent, man. Look at him."

"I don't have no $10,000 outfit, but I own half of Atlanta," Jay shot back.

Before the event, though, Jay had referenced the idea that finally meeting his rival face to face – or as face to face as anyone got during the pandemic – on an even playing field would bring them both a measure of peace and healing – and the same to their audience.

And, as often was the case with Jay's gut feelings, he turned out to be right.

In the end, after a furious few hours of spinning their tracks, the two joined together for the song that had started the rivalry long before at the beginnings of their careers. For the first time since the initial recording, Jay and Gucci Mane performed *So Icy* as a duo.

It may not have been a final covering-over of the past fifteen years, but it was enough to prove that both artists had set their beef aside at last.

Acknowledging the fact that it was Jay who had invited him to meet up for the Verzuz after all the hits were played, Mane told him, "I respect, I appreciate you for throwing out the olive branch. I accept that. No disrespect, it's all love."

For rappers with a years-long beef, that was as good as it was ever going to get.

CHAPTER 9

In early 2021, not long after the Verzuz battle that had set records for viewership, Sandra Jenkins passed away.

She had been ill for some time; Jay had made mention of it here and there in interviews, never wanting to say too much. It made him too emotional. Even the track he'd written for her, *The Real MVP*, he couldn't read over again without tears coming to his eyes. His mother had been a complicated part of his complicated life; he'd lost so much time that he should have had with her due to the tense relationship with his father, the way they'd moved around so much – and the drugs. Always it was the drugs that had torn them apart, and only coming clean had allowed them to mend together and be in each other's lives once more. He was grateful for what he'd had – though he missed her.

"One of the only people in the world I could trust,"

he wrote. "When I had nothing or no one, I had you, Mamma. You were hard on me. I thank you for that. You taught me to be a man when I was a boy. It made me man up to be a father when I was a kid. You lifted me when I was down. It inspired me when I had no inspiration. They always told me I was bigger than my circumstances. It made me feel like I could put the world on my back and walk barefoot."

Only a month afterward, carrying his mother's love with him, Jay married his long-time girlfriend, Jeannie Mai. They had been dating since 2018 and had been engaged for a year before finally deciding to go ahead with a small ceremony due to the pandemic. The couple had decided to create their own vows to reflect their love for each other. Later, Jeannie related with a laugh, "Everybody knows that I'm long-winded. So my vows were on three pages, and I read every word to him. Jay, he's a man of words. He's an artist, a songwriter, and he knows exactly how to describe what it feels like to marry me. Jay didn't write down his vows. He spoke them from the heart."

In all the relationships Jay Jenkins had gone through, even with the mothers of his children, he'd never had the settled, stable relationship, the depth of love and happiness that he found with his first marriage. Maybe it was about getting older. Maybe it was about re-evaluating the importance of the street cred he'd earned with blood, sweat, tears, and drugs.

Maybe it was about always evolving.

Jay Jenkins – the rapper formerly known as Lil J and Young Jeezy, the artist formally known as Jeezy today – isn't afraid of his past.

Even though there were certainly times that should have caused him to fear. As he grew older, he was able to look back and pinpoint some of the times when he came within a hair's breadth of falling victim to the consequences that caught so many of his friends. Living a life with street cred as king wasn't living much of a life at all. There were bigger things to achieve, a bigger picture to be seen.

And the best way he could help others to see it was through his music.

In an interview recently, he reminisced over his past and how it informed his future.

"My uncle used to pick me up back in the day in one of these old cars," he said. "And he's like, 'Get in the car, nephew, and let me tell you something.' We'd ride around the block, and by the time I'd get done listening to Curtis Mayfield, I felt like I could take the whole world. Because he put me in that passenger seat and took me around the block, and showed me what life was. And that's what I want to do. Music heals, and I want my music to be timeless. I'd rather be in the hearts and minds instead of on the shelves. I know I got love for this music 'cause it's a hustle." He paused, his familiar warm, wide smile stretching across his face. "There's a message in there, and I want people to hear it. I want each and every person to hop in that Delta '88 with me and spin a few blocks, and let's talk about what's going on out here."

Whatever comes next for Jay Jenkins, there's one thing for certain.

He's never going to stop the hustle.

Made in the USA
Las Vegas, NV
18 October 2023